THE ART OF WIRE WEAVING

A Beginner's Guide to Elegant Jewelry Designs

WALTER E. MATHIEU

Copyright © 2025

Table of contents

Introduction to Wire Weaving

What's Wire Weaving?

Wire weaving is an ancient craft that has stood the test of time, evolving from its roots in traditional jewelry-making to a modern art form that captivates both artisans and enthusiasts alike. This intricate technique involves intertwining fine wires to create beautiful, detailed patterns that can be transformed into stunning pieces of jewelry or decorative items.

Why Wire Weaving?

Wire weaving offers a unique blend of precision and creativity. It allows for the creation of complex, elegant designs without the need for soldering or advanced metalworking tools. The technique is versatile, enabling artists to experiment with various patterns, textures, and combinations of materials like beads, stones, and other embellishments.

The appeal of wire weaving lies in its accessibility and the sheer variety of outcomes it can produce. Whether you're crafting a delicate pair of earrings or a statement necklace, wire weaving provides endless possibilities for personal expression.

Overview of Techniques

At its core, wire weaving involves wrapping thinner wires around a base wire, interlacing them in specific patterns to create texture and structure. The basic techniques, such as single wire weaves or the figure-eight weave, form the foundation for more complex patterns. As you advance, you'll discover how to combine different weaves, incorporate beads, and experiment with various wire gauges to add depth and dimension to your work.

The Joy of Creation

Beyond the technical aspects, wire weaving is a deeply satisfying craft. The rhythmic motion of weaving wire can be meditative, and the transformation of simple materials into intricate designs brings a unique sense of accomplishment. As you progress, you'll find yourself developing a personal style, mastering techniques, and creating pieces that reflect your creativity and skill.

In this book, we'll journey together through the fundamentals of wire weaving, exploring both traditional and contemporary techniques. Whether you're just starting out or looking to refine your skills, you'll find this guide a comprehensive resource to help you create beautiful, hand-crafted wire jewelry.

CHAPTER 1

History and Origin of Wire Weaving

Wire weaving is one of the oldest forms of jewelry-making, with roots that stretch back thousands of years. This intricate art form has been practiced by various cultures, each contributing to its evolution and refinement.

Ancient Beginnings

The earliest evidence of wire weaving can be traced to ancient Mesopotamia and Egypt, where artisans used fine metal wires to create elaborate jewelry pieces. In these early civilizations, jewelry was not only a symbol of wealth and status but also a means of artistic expression. Gold and silver, prized for their malleability and luster, were commonly used in crafting these pieces.

The Egyptians

In ancient Egypt, wire weaving techniques were employed to produce intricate patterns in gold and silver jewelry. Egyptian artisans were known for their skill in metalworking, creating elaborate necklaces, bracelets, and rings. They often combined wire weaving with other techniques like granulation and filigree, adding a level of detail that is still admired today.

The Greeks and Romans

The art of wire weaving continued to flourish in ancient Greece and Rome. Greek jewelry, known for its elegance and refinement, often featured delicate wirework that complemented the use of gemstones and beads. The Romans, who inherited much of their jewelry-making knowledge from the Greeks, further developed these techniques, creating more robust and ornate designs.

The Middle Ages

During the Middle Ages, wire weaving techniques spread across Europe, becoming a staple in medieval jewelry. The method was used to create intricate chains and decorative elements for both religious artifacts and personal adornment. The craftsmanship of this period was heavily influenced by the church, with many pieces serving as symbols of faith and devotion.

The Renaissance and Beyond

The Renaissance period saw a resurgence in the arts, including jewelry-making. Wire weaving was refined further as artists experimented with new patterns and styles. This period marked the beginning of jewelry becoming more accessible to the growing middle class, rather than being reserved solely for the elite.

Modern Revival

The art of wire weaving experienced a revival in the 20th century, with the rise of the Arts and Crafts movement. This movement emphasized hand craftsmanship and traditional techniques, leading to renewed interest in wirework. Today, wire weaving has become a popular hobby and profession, embraced by jewelers and crafters around the world.

The evolution of wire weaving reflects a rich history of human creativity and adaptation. Each era and culture added layers of complexity and style, resulting in the diverse range of techniques and designs we have today.

This historical journey sets the stage for understanding the enduring appeal of wire weaving. As we delve into the techniques and projects in this book, you'll be part of a long tradition of artisans who have been inspired by the versatility and beauty of wire.

Application of Wire Weaving

Wire weaving is a versatile technique with applications that span across various forms of jewelry and decorative arts. Its adaptability and intricate patterns make it a favorite among artisans and crafters. Here are some of the most common and creative applications of wire weaving:

1. **Jewelry Making:** Wire weaving is primarily used in jewelry making, where its intricate patterns and designs add texture and elegance to pieces. Common applications include:

- **Earrings**: Wire weaving can be used to create delicate and intricate earrings, incorporating beads, stones, or simply showcasing the wirework itself.

- **Necklaces**: From simple pendants to elaborate statement pieces, wire weaving enhances the beauty of necklaces with its detailed designs.

- **Bracelets**: Whether a simple cuff or a complex bangle, wire weaving adds sophistication to wrist adornments.

- **Rings**: Wire weaving allows for the creation of unique and personalized rings, often featuring intricate patterns or incorporating gemstones.

2. **Decorative Art:** Beyond jewelry, wire weaving is also used in decorative arts, where it can transform simple objects into works of art:

- **Home Decor**: Wire weaving can be applied to create decorative items like picture frames, wall hangings, and sculptures, adding a touch of handcrafted elegance to home interiors.

- **Ornaments**: Seasonal decorations, such as Christmas ornaments or other holiday-themed items, can be beautifully crafted using wire weaving techniques.

3. **Fashion Accessories:** Wire weaving extends to fashion accessories beyond traditional jewelry, including:

- **Hair Accessories**: Hairpins, combs, and headbands can be adorned with wire weaving designs, offering unique and stylish options for hair embellishments.

- **Brooches**: Wire-woven brooches can serve as statement pieces that add flair to clothing or accessories.

4. Mixed Media Art

Wire weaving is often combined with other materials and techniques in mixed media art projects. This fusion allows for the creation of innovative and contemporary designs:

- **Textile Integration**: Wire weaving can be incorporated into fabric-based projects, such as clothing or bags, providing a striking contrast between soft textiles and rigid wire.

- **Beadwork and Gemstones**: The technique pairs beautifully with beadwork, allowing for the creation of intricate jewelry that combines the rigidity of wire with the color and texture of beads and gemstones.

5. **Functional Art:** Wire weaving also finds its place in creating functional art pieces that serve practical purposes while being aesthetically pleasing:

- **Jewelry Stands**: Wire-woven structures can be used as stands or holders for jewelry, blending function with artistic design.

- **Bookmarks**: Delicate wire-woven bookmarks make for elegant and thoughtful gifts, combining utility with beauty.

6. **Custom and Personalized Gifts:** The versatility of wire weaving makes it an excellent choice for creating custom and personalized gifts. Names, initials, or specific designs can be woven into jewelry or decor items, offering a unique and meaningful gift option.

Wire weaving is a craft that transcends mere ornamentation, turning everyday items into expressions of art and personal style. Its wide range of applications ensures that there is always something new to explore and create, making it a favorite among artisans and hobbyists alike.

Materials and Tools

To create beautiful wire-woven jewelry, it's essential to have the right materials and tools. This section covers the various types of wire, beads, and essential tools you'll need to get started and succeed in wire weaving.

Materials

1. Wire

- **Base Wire (16-20 gauge)**: Thicker wire used to create the structural framework for your projects. Choose from metals like copper, brass, sterling silver, or gold-filled wire, depending on your preference and budget.

- **Weaving Wire (26-30 gauge):** Thinner wire used for the intricate weaving patterns. It's flexible enough to weave around the base wire but strong enough to hold its shape.

2. Beads and Gemstones

- **Beads**: Available in various materials such as glass, ceramic, or metal, beads can add color and texture to your designs.

- **Gemstones**: Semi-precious stones, crystals, and pearls can be incorporated into your designs for an elegant touch.

3. Findings

- Jump Rings: Small metal rings used to connect different parts of your jewelry.

- **Clasps**: Used to secure necklaces, bracelets, and other types of jewelry.

- **Ear Wires**: Essential for making earrings.

4. Other Materials

- **Patina**: Used to create an aged or oxidized look on metals like copper or brass.
- Wire Coating: Clear coatings can protect your wire and prevent tarnishing.

Tools

1. **Cutting Tools**

   - **Wire Cutters**: Sharp cutters are essential for cleanly cutting through different gauges of wire.

2. **Pliers**

   - **Round Nose Pliers**: Used for creating loops and curves in the wire.

   - **Flat Nose Pliers**: Help in holding the wire firmly and making angular bends.

   - **Chain Nose Pliers**: Similar to flat nose pliers but with tapered tips, they're useful for intricate work.

- **Bent Nose Pliers**: Their angled tips make it easier to grip wire in tight spaces.

3. Shaping Tools

- **Mandrels**: Cylindrical rods used for shaping wire into uniform loops and coils. You can use a variety of mandrels like ring mandrels or smaller rods for different designs.

- **Jig:** A pegboard that helps in creating precise and repeatable patterns.

4. Finishing Tools
Files: Used to smooth sharp wire ends after cutting.

Polishing Cloths: Help in shining your finished pieces.

5. Measurement Tools

- **Ruler or Measuring Tape**: Essential for measuring the wire length accurately.

- **Caliper**: Useful for measuring the thickness of the wire and beads.

6. **Optional Tools**
    - **Soldering Kit**: For more advanced designs that require soldering.

    - **Torch**: Used in soldering or annealing wire to soften it.

    - **Tumbler**: A device used to polish and harden metal jewelry.

Having the right materials and tools is crucial for successful wire weaving. Investing in quality tools can make the process smoother and more enjoyable, while using the appropriate materials can enhance the durability and aesthetic of your finished pieces. As you progress in your wire weaving journey, you may find it useful to expand your toolkit and experiment with different materials to broaden your creative possibilities.

CHAPTER 2

Basic Techniques

As a beginner in wire weaving, you'll need to learn some basic techniques which will prepare you for advanced
Projects. Below are five basic techniques with steps and materials needed to master them:

Materials Needed for All Techniques

- **Base Wire**: Choose a thicker gauge (16-20) for the structure.
- **Weaving Wire**: A thinner gauge (24-28) for weaving patterns.
- **Wire Cutters**: For cutting the wire.
- **Chain Nose Pliers**: For holding and manipulating the wire.
- **Flat Nose Pliers**: For flattening and adjusting weaves.
- **Ruler**: For measuring wire lengths.
- **Beads (optional):** To add decorative elements.

Single Wire Weave

Steps:

1. Cut a piece of base wire to your desired length.
2. Cut a longer piece of thinner weaving wire (about five times the length of the base wire).
3. Secure the weaving wire by wrapping it tightly around the base wire three times.

4. Push the wraps close together using pliers or your fingers.

5. Continue wrapping the weaving wire around the base wire, keeping the wraps tight and evenly spaced.

6. Once you've covered the desired length, trim any excess wire and secure the ends by tucking them in with pliers.

Double Wire Weave

Steps:

1. Cut two pieces of base wire to the same length.

2. Cut a long piece of weaving wire.

3. Wrap the weaving wire around the first base wire three times to secure it.

4. Bring the weaving wire under the second base wire and wrap it around both wires once.

5. Continue by alternating wraps: once around the first wire, then around both wires together.

6. Repeat the pattern until you reach the desired length.

7. Trim and secure the ends as needed.

Figure-Eight Weave

Steps:

1. Cut two pieces of base wire.
2. Secure the weaving wire to one of the base wires with three wraps.
3. Pass the weaving wire over the first base wire, then under the second, and back over the second wire, forming a figure-eight pattern.
4. Continue the pattern, ensuring that each loop is tight and even.
5. Finish by securing the wire and trimming the excess.

Basket Weave

Steps:

1. Cut three pieces of base wire.
2. Secure the weaving wire to one of the outer base wires.
3. Weave over the first wire, under the second, and over the third, then back under the second and over the first, alternating with each pass.
4. Tighten each loop as you go along to maintain even spacing.

5. Continue weaving to the desired length, then secure and trim the wire.

Spiral Weave

Steps:

1. Cut a piece of base wire.
2. Cut a long piece of weaving wire and secure it to the base wire with three wraps.
3. Wrap the weaving wire around the base wire three times, then slide the wraps slightly to form a spiral shape.

4. Continue wrapping, keeping the spirals evenly spaced.

5. Secure and trim the excess wire at the end.

These basic techniques are the building blocks for more complex wire weaving designs. Practice each technique to master the foundational skills, and you'll soon be able to combine them into intricate and beautiful wire-woven creations.

CHAPTER 3

Intermediate Techniques

Once you've mastered the basics, it's time to expand your skills with intermediate techniques. These methods build on the foundational wire weaving techniques and introduce more complexity, incorporating different patterns, textures, and embellishments.

Materials Needed for All Techniques

- **Base Wire**: Choose thicker gauges (18-22) for structure.
- **Weaving Wire**: A thinner gauge (26-30) for weaving.
- **Wire Cutters**: To cut the wire.
- **Chain Nose Pliers**: To manipulate and tighten the wire.
- **Round Nose Pliers**: To create loops or curves in the wire.
- **Flat Nose Pliers**: For flattening and adjusting the weave.

- **Beads or Gemstones (optional):** To embellish designs.

Captive Wire Weave

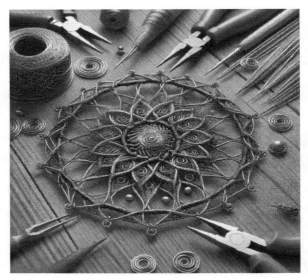

Steps:

1. **Prepare the Base Wire**: Cut two pieces of base wire—one will form the core, and the other will act as the weaving wire.
2. **Anchor the Weaving Wire**: Begin by anchoring the weaving wire around the base wire in a simple loop, wrapping it around the wire three times to secure it.

3. **Weave the Wire**: Wrap the weaving wire around the base wire in a circular pattern, ensuring that the wire loops captively around the core wire.

4. **Create Captive Loops**: Continue weaving until you have enough length to form a loop or section where the weaving wire encircles the base wire in multiple loops.

5. **Finish the Weave**: Once you've completed the desired section, secure the ends of the weaving wire by tucking them in with pliers.

Trillion Weave

Steps:

1. **Prepare the Base Wire**: Cut three pieces of wire (usually 18 gauge) for the base. The wires should be of equal length.
2. **Position the Wires**: Lay the three wires next to each other, arranging them in a triangular shape.
3. **Start Weaving**: Using a thinner wire (24-26 gauge), start by weaving around the outer wires in a spiral or zigzag pattern, working your way along the entire base.

4. **Continue Weaving**: As you weave, ensure that the center remains open to allow for the desired pattern to form. Continue this until you reach the end of the piece.

5. **Secure the Ends**: Once you reach the end, carefully secure the loose ends of the weaving wire with pliers and trim excess wire.

Double Spiral Weave

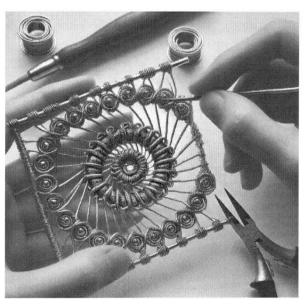

Steps:

1. **Prepare the Base Wire**: Cut two pieces of base wire (16-18 gauge). These will form the framework for the weave.

2. **Anchor the Weaving Wire**: Begin by securing a thinner weaving wire (24-26 gauge) to one of the base wires with a few wraps.

3. **Start the Spiral Weave**: Weave the wire around both base wires, spiraling outward in a double helix pattern. Ensure that each wrap is tight and even.

4. **Increase the Spiral**: As you move along, increase the distance between each spiral to create a wide, flowing double spiral.

5. **Secure the Ends**: Finish by securing the ends of the weaving wire neatly and trim any excess.

Zigzag Weave

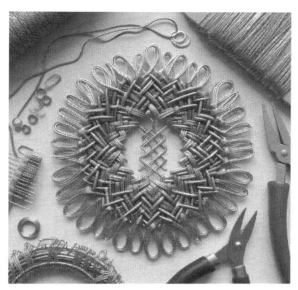

Steps:

1. **Prepare the Base Wire**: Cut a single piece of base wire (16-18 gauge) for the structure.

2. **Weaving Wire**: Use a thinner wire (24-26 gauge) and secure it to the base wire by making a few wraps at the starting point.

3. **Create Zigzag Pattern**: Begin weaving by passing the wire over and under the base wire at an angle, forming a series of zigzag loops along the wire.

4. **Continue Weaving**: As you continue, maintain the regularity of the zigzag pattern, ensuring the wire remains taut and evenly spaced.

5. **Finish**: Once you've completed the desired section, secure the weaving wire and trim any excess.

Rope Weave

Steps:

1. **Prepare the Base Wire**: Cut two pieces of base wire, typically 16-18 gauge.

2. Anchor the Weaving Wire: Secure a thinner weaving wire (24-28 gauge) to one of the base wires with three wraps.

3. **Begin Weaving:** Start by wrapping the weaving wire around both base wires in an alternating fashion, moving from one wire to the other.

4. **Create the Rope Effect**: As you continue weaving, twist the wire in a rope-like fashion to create a spiral effect. Ensure the wire is tightly wrapped and evenly spaced.

5. **Finish and Secure**: When you've reached the desired length, finish the weave and secure the ends of the wire by tucking them in with pliers.

These intermediate techniques build on the basics and open the door to more intricate and beautiful wire weaving patterns. With a bit of practice, you'll be able to create professional-quality wire jewelry and decorative pieces that showcase your evolving skills. Each of these techniques can be customized by adding beads, gemstones, or varying the wire gauges to achieve different effects.

CHAPTER 4

Advanced Techniques

After mastering basic and intermediate wire weaving techniques, you can challenge yourself with more advanced techniques. These techniques combine creativity with skill and allow for the creation of intricate, professional-level wire-woven jewelry and art pieces. Here's a guide to five advanced wire weaving techniques.

Materials Needed for All Techniques

- **Base Wire:** Choose gauges (18-22) for structural strength.
- **Weaving Wire**: A thinner gauge (26-30) for weaving.
- **Wire Cutters**: For cutting wire.
- **Chain Nose Pliers**: For manipulation and adjusting tightness.
- **Round Nose Pliers**: To create loops and curves in the wire.
- **Flat Nose Pliers**: For flattening and adjusting the weave.

- **Beads or Gemstones (optional)**: To embellish and enhance designs.

Basket Weave with Beads

Steps:

1. **Prepare the Base Wire**: Cut four pieces of base wire (18-22 gauge) to the desired length.
2. **Position the Base Wire**: Arrange the base wires in a parallel manner, ensuring there is space between each wire for weaving.

3. **Anchor the Weaving Wire**: Attach a thinner weaving wire (24-26 gauge) at one end and secure it with a few wraps around the base wires.

4. **Start Weaving**: Begin weaving by passing the weaving wire over and under the base wires, creating a basket-like grid pattern.

5. **Add Beads**: After weaving a few rows, thread a bead onto the weaving wire and continue weaving. The bead will be incorporated into the design, held in place by the wire.

6. **Continue Weaving**: Keep weaving, adding beads at regular intervals to create a textured, embellished effect.

7. **Secure the Ends**: Once you've finished the desired section, secure the loose ends of the weaving wire by tucking them in neatly with pliers.

Fused Wire Weaving

Steps:

1. **Prepare the Base Wire**: Cut several pieces of wire (18-22 gauge) for the base. You may want to use silver, copper, or brass for a fused effect.

2. **Start by Weaving**: Use a thinner weaving wire (26-30 gauge) to begin weaving over and under the base wires in a traditional weave pattern (such as a figure-eight or basket weave).

3. **Fuse the Wire**: Once you've completed a few sections of weaving, use a torch or soldering iron to fuse the wire ends together. Be careful not to melt the entire piece; just the ends of the wire should fuse.

4. **Continue Weaving and Fusing:** Continue weaving sections and fusing periodically to create a welded, seamless appearance.

5. **Finish the Design**: Once the design is complete, carefully clean and polish the piece.

Wire Crochet Weave

Steps:

1. **Prepare the Wire**: Choose a thin, flexible wire (26-30 gauge). Cut several lengths of wire for the crochet.

2. **Create the Foundation Chain**: Use a crochet hook (size 00-4) to create a simple chain of wire, with each stitch securely looped around the hook.

3. **Begin Crochet Weaving**: Continue the crochet process, adding more loops to create a mesh-like structure. You can use various crochet stitches such as single crochet or double crochet to create a more textured effect.

4. **Add Beads (Optional)**: For an added effect, add beads onto the wire during the crochet process by threading them onto the wire before making each stitch.

5. **Shape the Piece**: Once you've completed the crochet, gently shape the wire into the desired form (bracelet, necklace, etc.). Secure the ends with a loop or clasp.

Dragonfly Weave

Steps:

1. **Prepare the Base Wire**: Cut two pieces of base wire (18-20 gauge) for the main structure.
2. **Anchor the Weaving Wire**: Cut a thin weaving wire (24-26 gauge) and attach it to the base wires by wrapping it around them to secure.
3. **Create the Dragonfly Wings**: Start weaving the thin wire around the two base wires to create the wings of the dragonfly. The design consists of multiple loops and

twists that radiate outward from the center of the base wire.

4. **Add Details**: Weave additional small wire loops around the central body to form the dragonfly's legs and head.

5. **Finish the Weave**: Secure all ends of the weaving wire and trim any excess. Optionally, add small beads or gemstone eyes for decoration.

Coil and Weave

Steps:

1. **Prepare the Base Wire**: Cut several pieces of base wire (18-22 gauge) to form the frame of your design.

2. **Create the Coils**: Using a thicker gauge wire (22-24 gauge), coil it tightly around a mandrel or dowel rod. The coils should be uniform in size and spaced evenly.

3. **Weave the Wire**: Begin weaving a thinner wire (26-30 gauge) around the coils, weaving over and under each coil to create a pattern. You can form spirals or other intricate designs using this technique.

4. **Tighten the Coils**: Ensure the coils stay tight and secure as you continue weaving. Use pliers to tighten the coils where necessary.

5. **Finish the Piece**: Once you have achieved the desired pattern, finish the ends of the wire and secure them by tucking them into the weave or using a clasp.

These advanced wire weaving techniques require skill, patience, and creativity. They allow you to create intricate, professional designs with a high level of detail and personalization. As you continue to practice these advanced techniques, you'll be able to incorporate more complex elements into your work, such as adding gemstones, intricate textures, and unique patterns.

Tips for Success

Wire weaving is a highly creative and rewarding craft, but achieving professional-looking, durable, and intricate designs requires practice and attention to detail. Here are some tips to help you succeed in wire weaving and elevate your craft to the next level.

1. Use High-Quality Materials

- **Wire Quality**: Invest in good-quality wire, such as sterling silver, copper, or brass. Lower-quality wire may be harder to work with and could cause the finished piece to lose its integrity over time.

- **Choose the Right Gauge**: Select wire gauges that suit your design. Thicker wire (18-22 gauge) is great for structure and frames, while thinner wire (26-30 gauge) is best for weaving and intricate patterns.

- **Ensure Proper Wire Flexibility**: For weaving, it's important to use wire that is flexible enough to bend easily but also strong enough to hold its shape.

2. Practice Consistency

- **Maintain Even Tension**: Keep the tension consistent while weaving. Too tight and the wire may break or distort; too loose and the weave may appear uneven or loose.
- **Even Spacing**: When wrapping wire around the base, ensure the wraps are evenly spaced and aligned. This will give your design a uniform, professional appearance.

- **Use a Template**: If you're creating a specific shape or design, consider using a template to keep the dimensions consistent.

3. Organize Your Work Area

- **Keep Tools and Materials Accessible**: Having a clean, organized workspace will help you work more efficiently. Place your tools (pliers, wire cutters, etc.) and materials (wires, beads, etc.) within easy reach.

- **Use Wire Holders**: If you're working with long wire lengths, consider using a wire spool holder to avoid tangling and to keep your wire neat as you work.

4. **Secure the Ends Properly**

- **Avoid Sharp Edges**: Always ensure that the wire ends are properly tucked in or secured to avoid sharp edges that could scratch skin or damage the piece.

- **Use Pliers for Neat Finishes**: Use flat-nose or chain-nose pliers to tuck in any excess wire securely. You can also flatten the ends to prevent them from sticking out.

- **Hide the Ends**: For a cleaner, more polished look, hide the wire ends within the weave or use beads to cover them up.

5. Experiment with Different Techniques

- **Mix Weaving Patterns**: Don't be afraid to combine different weaving techniques in a single project. Mixing basic weaves like figure-eight, basket, and spiral patterns can result in stunning, one-of-a-kind designs.

- **Incorporate Other Elements**: Experiment by adding beads, gemstones, or even small wire coils to enhance the design. These additions can give your project texture, color, and visual interest.

6. Work Slowly and materials Methodically

- **Take Your Time**: Wire weaving can be intricate and time-consuming. Take your time to ensure each step is done properly and with care.

- **Avoid Rushing**: Rushing may cause mistakes such as uneven tension, loose wraps, or breaks in the wire. Patience is key to achieving a professional finish.

7. **Develop Your Eye for Design**

- **Plan Your Design**: Before starting a new project, sketch out the design and visualize how the weave will flow. This helps avoid mistakes and ensures a smooth process.

- **Experiment with Shapes**: Wire weaving allows you to create both geometric and organic shapes. Experiment with different forms, such as spirals, loops, and curves, to add variety to your designs.
- **Use Negative Space**: Don't be afraid of leaving some space open in your design. Negative space can create

balance and allow the intricate weaving to stand out.

8. Protect Your Hands and Tools

- **Use Proper Pliers**: Using the right pliers for each job will reduce strain on your hands and ensure a more controlled, precise result. Round nose pliers are ideal for making loops, while flat nose pliers are great for manipulating wire into shapes.

- **Wear Safety Gear**: Always wear safety glasses when using tools like wire cutters or a torch to protect your eyes from flying wire fragments or heat.

9. Polish and Finish Your Work

- Clean the Wire: After completing your piece, clean the wire to remove any fingerprints, oils, or tarnish. Use a polishing cloth or an ultrasonic cleaner if you have one.

- **Apply a Patina**: For a vintage or antique look, use a patina solution to darken the wire and give it a rustic feel. Just be sure to seal the patina to prevent further tarnishing.

- **Final Touches**: Consider adding clasps, jump rings, or other finishing hardware to complete the piece and ensure it's ready for wear or sale.

10. Troubleshoot Common Issues

- **Wire Breakage**: If your wire keeps breaking, ensure you're not pulling too tightly or using too thin a gauge. Consider using wire with more flexibility or using more wraps for added strength.

- **Uneven Weaves**: If the weave looks uneven, check the tension of each wrap and adjust the spacing. Using a small ruler to measure can help with consistency.

- **Loose Wrapping**: If the weave feels too loose, try tightening the wraps or using a thicker weaving wire to add more structure.

By following these tips and constantly practicing, you'll be able to create more intricate, polished, and professional wire woven pieces. Remember, mastery comes with patience and repetition. Embrace the process, experiment with new techniques, and always be open to learning from each project you complete!

CHAPTER 5

Beginner Project

If you're just starting out in wire weaving, it's essential to begin with simple projects that allow you to practice basic techniques while still creating beautiful pieces. Below are five beginner-friendly wire weaving projects that will help you build your skills while having fun crafting.

Materials Needed for All Projects

- **Base Wire**: 18-22 gauge wire (copper, silver, or brass)
- **Weaving Wire**: 26-30 gauge wire
- **Wire Cutters**: For cutting wire
- **Round Nose Pliers**: For creating loops and curves
- **Flat Nose Pliers**: For holding and bending wire
- **Chain Nose Pliers**: For making precise adjustments
- **Beads (optional)**: For embellishment

- **Mandrel or Pen**: For creating loops and curves (if required)
- **Clasp (optional)**: For finishing projects such as bracelets

Simple Wire-Wrapped Ring

Steps:

1. **Cut the Base Wire**: Cut a piece of 18-22 gauge wire about 6-8 inches long.
2. **Form the Ring Shape**: Using round nose pliers, make a small loop at one end of the

wire. Begin wrapping the wire around a mandrel or pen to form a ring shape, adjusting it to fit your finger.

3. **Add Decorative Elements**: Using the thinner weaving wire (26-30 gauge), wrap the wire around the base ring to create decorative loops or spirals. Optionally, add small beads to the weaving wire.

4. **Secure the Ends**: Use flat nose pliers to tuck in any loose ends of wire neatly against the band.

5. **Finish the Ring**: Once the desired design is complete, make sure the ring is comfortable to wear and that there are no sharp edges. If desired, add a clasp for adjustable sizing.

Wire-Wrapped Pendant

Steps:

1. **Cut the Base Wire**: Start with 12-16 inches of 18-22 gauge wire, depending on the size of your pendant.

2. **Form the Base Frame**: Use round nose pliers to create a loop at one end of the wire, then wrap the wire around itself to form a teardrop, oval, or circular shape. This will be the frame for your pendant.

3. **Add Decorative Weaving**: Take a thinner weaving wire (26-30 gauge) and

start weaving around the base frame in a crisscross or spiral pattern.

4. **Insert a Gemstone or Bead**: If you're adding a gemstone or bead, carefully place it in the center of the frame and continue weaving around it, securing the stone in place.

5. **Finish the Pendant**: Once you've finished weaving, tuck in the wire ends and attach a jump ring at the top for a necklace chain.

Wire-Wrapped Bracelet

Steps:

1. **Prepare the Base Wire**: Cut two lengths of 18-22 gauge wire, each about 7-8 inches long, for the bracelet's base.
2. **Create the Base Shape**: Use round nose pliers to form small loops at both ends of each piece of wire. Bend the wires to fit the desired bracelet size.
3. **Start Weaving**: Cut a piece of 26-30 gauge weaving wire and begin wrapping it around the base wires, creating simple weave patterns like the figure-eight or diagonal weave.
4. **Add Beads or Charms**: If desired, incorporate beads into the weave, either by threading them onto the wire or by wrapping around them.
5. **Secure the Ends and Attach the Clasp**: Use chain nose pliers to secure the loose ends of the wire. Attach a clasp to the bracelet to finish the piece.

Simple Wire Earrings

Steps:

1. Cut the Base Wire: Cut two pieces of 18-22 gauge wire, each about 4-6 inches long, for each earring.
2. Shape the Earrings: Using round nose pliers, form the wire into a simple loop or teardrop shape. If you want more intricate designs, try adding additional loops or swirls to the frame.
3. **Add Weaving**: Use a thinner weaving wire (26-30 gauge) to wrap the frame,

creating texture or designs such as spirals or swirls around the base wire.

4. **Add Beads (Optional)**: If desired, add small beads along the wire weave or at the center of the design.

5. **Finish the Earrings**: Attach an earring hook or wire to the top of the frame, and ensure the ends are neatly tucked in with flat nose pliers.

Wire-Wrapped Keychain

Steps:

1. **Cut the Base Wire**: Start with a 12-16 inch piece of 18-22 gauge wire.
2. **Form the Base Shape**: Use round nose pliers to create a loop at one end of the wire. Then bend the wire into a simple shape like a circle, square, or heart.
3. **Start Weaving**: Use a thinner 26-30 gauge wire to begin weaving around the base shape, incorporating spirals, figure-eights, or other simple patterns.
4. **Add a Charm or Bead**: If desired, add a small charm or bead to the design. You can secure the charm in place by weaving around it or using jump rings.
5. **Attach to Keychain**: Attach the completed wire design to a keychain ring using a jump ring, and use chain nose pliers to secure everything tightly.

These five beginner projects offer a great starting point for learning wire weaving. Each project helps you master a new skill, whether it's forming shapes, adding beads, or incorporating different weaving techniques. As you work through these projects, you'll build the foundational skills needed to tackle more advanced designs.

CHAPTER 6

Intermediate Project

As you progress in your wire weaving journey, intermediate projects allow you to experiment with more complex techniques and designs. These projects will help you refine your skills while creating stunning, intricate pieces. Below are five intermediate wire weaving projects to elevate your craft.

Materials Needed for All Projects

- **Base Wire**: 18-22 gauge wire (copper, sterling silver, or brass)
- **Weaving Wire**: 26-30 gauge wire
- **Wire Cutters**: For cutting wire
- **Round Nose Pliers**: For creating loops and curves
- **Flat Nose Pliers**: For holding and bending wire
- **Chain Nose Pliers**: For making precise adjustments
- **Beads (optional)**: For embellishment

- **Mandrel or Pen**: For creating loops and curves (if required)
- **Jump Rings and Clasps**: For finishing projects like pendants, earrings, or bracelets

Wire-Wrapped Cabochon Pendant

Steps:

1. **Prepare the Base Wire**: Cut a piece of 18-22 gauge wire, approximately 10-12

inches, to create the frame for your cabochon.

2. **Shape the Frame**: Use round nose pliers to make a loop at the top of the wire. Bend the wire into a circular or oval shape to fit your cabochon.

3. **Secure the Cabochon**: Place the cabochon in the center of the frame. Begin wrapping the base wire around the stone to secure it, using a simple weave or pattern to hold the cabochon in place.

4. **Add Weaving Wire**: Take 26-30 gauge weaving wire and begin weaving around the frame, creating a decorative weave pattern around the cabochon. You can add small beads to the weaving wire for extra embellishment.

5. **Finish the Pendant**: Once the cabochon is securely wrapped, use flat nose pliers to tuck in any loose ends. Attach a jump ring to the top of the pendant for a necklace chain.

Wire-Wrapped Bead and Wire Bracelet

Steps:

1. **Prepare the Base Wire**: Cut two pieces of 18-22 gauge wire, each about 7-8 inches long, for the bracelet's base.
2. **Form the Base Shape**: Shape each wire into a cuff, bending them into an oval or circular shape to fit around your wrist. Leave some space between the two wires to weave beads into the bracelet.

3. **Weave with Beads**: Cut a piece of 26-30 gauge wire, and begin weaving around both base wires, placing beads at regular intervals. You can use round or faceted beads for added texture and visual interest.

4. **Add Decorative Weave**: Once the beads are in place, continue weaving around the base to create a more intricate pattern, like a spiral or basket weave.

5. **Finish the Bracelet**: Secure the wire ends, making sure there are no sharp edges. Attach a clasp to the bracelet to make it adjustable and easy to wear.

Wire-Wrapped Tree of Life Pendant

Steps:

1. **Prepare the Base Wire**: Cut 16-18 gauge wire, about 12-14 inches long, to form the Tree of Life frame. You'll need additional 26-30 gauge wire for weaving.
2. **Form the Frame**: Use round nose pliers to create a small loop at the top of the wire. Bend the wire into a circle (about 2-3 inches in diameter) to form the base of the tree.

3. **Add the Tree Roots**: Begin weaving the bottom part of the circle to create "roots" for the tree. Use weaving wire (26-30 gauge) to create a textured, root-like pattern.

4. **Create the Tree Trunk and Branches**: For the trunk, take the thicker wire and create small branches by bending and weaving them outward from the center. Add weaving wire to create texture around the branches.

5. **Finish the Pendant**: Once the tree is complete, tidy up any wire ends and add a jump ring at the top for hanging the pendant on a necklace.

Wire-Wrapped Bead Cluster Earrings

Steps:

1. **Prepare the Base Wire**: Cut two pieces of 20-22 gauge wire, about 4-6 inches long.

2. **Form the Earring Frame**: Use round nose pliers to form small hoops or teardrop shapes. These will serve as the base of your earrings.

3. **Add Bead Clusters**: Take a thinner 26-30 gauge wire and thread small beads (such as seed beads, pearls, or crystals) onto the

wire. Twist the wire around the base wire to secure the beads into a cluster formation.

4. **Weave for Texture**: Once the bead clusters are attached, use weaving wire to create texture around the frame, such as a simple spiral or crisscross pattern.

5. **Finish the Earrings**: After the design is complete, attach an earring hook to the top loop of the frame and secure all loose wire ends.

Wire-Wrapped Gemstone Ring

Steps:

1. **Prepare the Base Wire**: Cut a piece of 18-20 gauge wire, about 6-8 inches long, to form the ring band.

2. **Form the Ring Band**: Use round nose pliers to create a small loop at one end. Wrap the wire around a mandrel or your finger to create a ring band that fits comfortably.

3. **Create a Gemstone Setting**: For the setting, cut another piece of wire (about 10 inches). Use round nose pliers to form loops at both ends of the wire. Bend the wire into a shape that will hold your gemstone securely in place.

4. **Weave the Setting**: Using 26-30 gauge wire, weave around the gemstone setting, securing the stone in place and adding decorative weaving patterns around the base.

5. **Finish the Ring**: Once the gemstone is securely set, use flat nose pliers to tuck in any loose wire ends. Attach the gemstone setting to the ring band, securing it tightly.

These intermediate wire weaving projects help you build on basic skills while allowing you to experiment with more intricate designs and techniques. They will give you the chance to work with different types of wire, incorporate beads and gemstones, and refine your weaving methods. As you complete these projects, you'll gain the confidence to move on to even more advanced wire weaving designs.

CHAPTER 7

Advanced Project

As you advance in your wire weaving journey, you'll begin to explore more complex techniques, including intricate designs, advanced gemstone settings, and multi-layered wire combinations. These projects are designed to challenge your skills and take your wire weaving to the next level.

Materials Needed for All Projects

- **Base Wire**: 16-20 gauge wire (copper, sterling silver, or brass)
- **Weaving Wire**: 26-30 gauge wire
- **Wire Cutters**: For cutting wire
- **Round Nose Pliers**: For creating loops and curves
- **Flat Nose Pliers**: For holding and bending wire
- **Chain Nose Pliers**: For precise adjustments

- **Beads and Gemstones**: Semi-precious stones, pearls, crystals, or other decorative beads
- **Mandrel or Pen**: For shaping wire (if needed)
- **Jump Rings and Clasps**: For finishing projects such as pendants, earrings, or bracelets
- Soldering Kit (optional for some projects)
- **Patina (optional):** For adding an aged effect to your wire pieces

Multi-Point Gemstone Pendant

Steps:

1. **Prepare the Base Wire**: Cut several pieces of 18-20 gauge wire, each about 8-10 inches long. These will form the structure of your pendant.

2. **Create the Frame**: Begin by forming a circular or oval frame with round nose pliers. You can also create a more complex multi-pointed design by bending the wire at different angles and securing the ends with pliers.

3. **Place Gemstones**: Select multiple small gemstones or beads to be placed at various points of the pendant. Wrap them tightly in place, ensuring they are securely fixed with weaving wire.

4. **Start Weaving**: Take 26-30 gauge weaving wire and begin weaving around the frame, incorporating the gemstones into the weave. You can create an intricate crisscross pattern or add spirals between the stones for added texture.

5. **Finish the Pendant**: After securing the gemstones, add a jump ring at the top for hanging and make sure all loose ends are

tucked in securely. You can use patina to add an aged look if desired.

Wire-Wrapped Caged Pendant with Multiple Stones

Steps:

1. **Prepare the Base Wire**: Cut several pieces of 16-18 gauge wire for the base cage. You'll need about 12-14 inches of wire.
2. **Form the Cage Frame**: Begin by creating a simple round or oval frame using

round nose pliers. Then, start wrapping the wire around itself to form a cage that will hold your stones.

3. **Position the Stones**: Choose several small gemstones or crystals. Begin placing the stones inside the cage and wrap the base wire around them, ensuring they are securely held within the cage structure.

4. **Weave for Texture**: Using 26-30 gauge wire, start weaving around the base frame and stones, filling any gaps and creating a textured pattern around the cage.

5. **Finish the Pendant**: After securing all stones, trim any excess wire and attach a jump ring at the top for hanging the pendant.

Wire-Wrapped Bracelet with Adjustable Cuff Design

Steps:

1. **Prepare the Base Wire**: Cut two pieces of 16-18 gauge wire, each about 8-10 inches long. These will form the cuff part of the bracelet.

2. **Shape the Cuff**: Use round nose pliers to form each wire into a cuff shape that fits around your wrist.

3. **Add Gemstone or Bead Elements**: Select several beads or gemstones that you

want to incorporate into the design. Position them at desired intervals along the cuff and secure them in place with thin wire.

4. **Create Decorative Weaving**: Using 26-30 gauge wire, begin weaving around the cuff, integrating beads or gemstones as you go. You can use various weaving patterns such as the figure-eight or basket weave.

5. **Finish the Bracelet**: Once you've completed the weaving, secure the wire ends and attach a clasp to the cuff for easy wear.

Wire-Wrapped Mandala Pendant

Steps:

1. **Prepare the Base Wire**: Cut a piece of 18-20 gauge wire, about 10-12 inches long, for the circular frame.
2. **Create the Frame**: Use round nose pliers to form a circular or mandala shape. This will serve as the base for your design.
3. **Add Weaving Structure**: Using 26-30 gauge wire, start weaving intricate geometric patterns inside the frame. You can create radiating lines, spirals, or other mandala-inspired designs.
4. **Incorporate Stones or Beads**: Add small beads or gemstones at key intersections within the mandala, using weaving wire to hold them in place.
5. **Finish the Pendant**: Once the weaving is complete, ensure all loose ends are tucked in securely. Attach a jump ring for hanging the mandala pendant.

Wire-Wrapped Sculptural Necklace with Multiple Elements

Steps:

1. **Prepare the Base Wire**: Cut several pieces of 16-18 gauge wire, each about 12-14 inches long. These will serve as the base for various components of the necklace.

2. **Create Sculptural Elements**: Use round nose pliers and flat nose pliers to create intricate loops, swirls, and other sculptural elements. Combine them to form the centerpiece of the necklace.

3. **Add Beads and Gemstones**: Select a variety of beads and gemstones. Begin attaching them to the sculptural elements by wrapping them with weaving wire, making sure they are securely fixed.

4. **Weave Decorative Details**: Using 26-30 gauge wire, weave around the base wires, adding texture and detail to the sculptural elements. This step involves layering the wire and beads to build up complexity.

5. **Assemble the Necklace**: Once all sculptural elements are woven together and secured, attach them to a chain or cord. Finish the necklace with a clasp to make it wearable.

These advanced wire weaving projects will push your creativity and technical ability to new heights. By combining different techniques like sculpting, weaving, and stone setting, you'll be able to craft intricate, multi-dimensional pieces of jewelry that showcase your advanced wire weaving skills. Each project requires patience and precision, but the results will be beautiful, high-quality pieces that demonstrate the full extent of your wire weaving abilities

Troubleshooting and Solutions

Wire weaving can be a rewarding and creative craft, but like any skill, it comes with its own set of challenges. Below is a guide to common problems you may encounter while wire weaving and practical solutions to address them.

1. **Wire is Too Soft or Too Hard**

Problem:
- **Too Soft**: Soft wire (often due to a low gauge or low-quality metal) may bend too easily, making it difficult to work with for intricate designs.

- **Too Hard**: Hard wire can be difficult to manipulate and may break when too much pressure is applied.

Solutions:

- **Too Soft**: Opt for a stronger wire, such as half-hard or hard-temper wire, which retains its shape better but still allows for manipulation. If you must use soft wire, consider using smaller pieces and reinforcing them with additional wire.

- **Too Hard**: If the wire is too stiff to work with, gently anneal the wire (heat it with a torch and then cool it down slowly) to soften it. You can also use a larger gauge (thicker) wire if you're working on larger pieces, or consider switching to a lower gauge to give the wire more flexibility.

2. **Wire Gets Tangled or Knotted**

Problem: Wire can sometimes become tangled or knotted, especially when handling longer lengths or working on intricate designs.

Solutions:

- **Preventing Tangles**: When pulling wire from the spool, make sure to straighten it by pulling it gently along a flat surface. Keep your working area tidy, and always organize the wire in manageable lengths (around 8-12 inches) when working on smaller sections.

- **Untangling**: If wire tangles, carefully work it loose using flat nose pliers, or cut the tangled section and start fresh. For finer gauges, use a gentle approach to avoid kinking the wire.

3. **Weaving Wire Slips or Doesn't Stay Tight**

Problem: When weaving with smaller wire gauges, the weaving wire can slip or become loose, especially if you're working with a fine weave or larger project.

Solutions:

- **Tension**: Maintain consistent tension while weaving. If the wire is too loose, pull slightly tighter when weaving, but don't overtighten, as this can distort the wire's shape or cause it to snap.

- **Use a Tension Board**: Consider using a tension board to keep your project taut as you weave. This allows you to maintain consistent pressure and prevents the weaving wire from loosening.

- **Pinning**: For more complex projects, you can pin the weaving in place on a corkboard or similar surface to prevent slipping.

4. **Wire Ends are Sharp or Rough**

Problem: After completing a project, sharp wire ends can be uncomfortable to wear and may pose a risk of injury.

Solutions:

- **Tuck Ends In**: Always use flat nose pliers to tuck wire ends in neatly into the woven sections. This keeps the ends smooth and prevents them from sticking out.

- **File the Ends**: For extra smoothness, use a wire file to file down sharp ends after cutting the wire. This is especially important when working with fine wires like sterling silver or gold-filled wire.

- **Use a Patina or Finish**: If you're working with wire that is prone to tarnishing or has rough edges, applying a protective patina or using a wire finishing product (such as a metal polish or coating) can also help smooth and protect the wire ends.

5. Wire Does Not Hold the Shape

Problem: Sometimes wire won't hold the shape you want, whether you're trying to make loops, coils, or curves. This can happen due to wire tension, gauge, or poor design structure.

Solutions:

- **Proper Gauge**: Ensure that you're using the correct gauge wire for the type of project. Thicker gauges (16-18) are better for creating structural components like frames, while finer gauges (26-30) work better for weaving and embellishments.

- **Annealing**: If you're working with a particularly stubborn wire, annealing it (heating it and then allowing it to cool) can make it more malleable and easier to manipulate.

- **Use Tools**: For precise shaping, use mandrels, pliers, or dowels to help maintain your curves and loops. These tools ensure that you create consistent shapes that hold their form.

6. **Uneven Weaving or Inconsistent Patterns**

Problem: Inconsistent weaving patterns or uneven tension can result in an uneven design, causing your project to look misaligned or chaotic.

Solutions:

- **Even Tension**: Work on maintaining even tension throughout the project. If the wire is too loose or tight in spots, it can cause irregularities. Be mindful of your grip and make slight adjustments with your pliers as you go.

- **Keep the Pattern Simple**: If you're just starting to notice unevenness, simplify the pattern. Complex weaves can be harder to maintain consistently, so start with simpler weaves until you get the hang of even tension.

- **Use a Template**: For highly intricate designs, consider using a template or drawing the pattern on paper first. You can also use a beadboard or board with measured segments to guide your weaving.

7. Soldering Problems (if applicable)

Problem: If you're using soldering in your wire weaving, problems like poor adhesion, excessive solder flow, or oxidation can arise.

Solutions:

- **Clean the Surface**: Always clean the wire and surfaces you plan to solder. Use a pickling solution or abrasive pad to remove oxidation and oils.

- **Proper Heat**: Be sure to use the appropriate amount of heat. Too much heat can melt the wire, while too little may prevent the solder from bonding properly.

- **Pickling Solution**: After soldering, use a pickling solution (such as citric acid or commercial pickle) to clean off any residual flux or oxidation from the wire.

8. Design Feels Too Loose or Too Tight

Problem: Sometimes, your wire weaving can end up too tight (resulting in a stiff, uncomfortable piece) or too loose (causing the design to lose structure).

Solutions:

- **Adjust Tension**: Tighten or loosen the tension of the wire as you work. For a flexible design, aim for slightly looser tension, whereas for a stiffer structure, use tighter tension.

- **Fit and Comfort**: If you're working on a wearable item like a ring or bracelet, measure the wire around your wrist or finger and periodically check that the piece fits comfortably. If it's too tight, loosen the weave and vice versa.

9. **Misalignment of Beads or Stones**

Problem: When incorporating beads or stones, they may not align perfectly, making the finished product look unbalanced.

Solutions:

- **Plan the Layout**: Before securing the beads or stones, lay them out on your project and experiment with the placement until you find an arrangement that looks balanced.

- **Adjust the Wire Tension**: Slightly adjust the tension of the wire on either side of a bead or stone to make sure it sits exactly where you want it. This will help keep the beads in place.

- **Use Bead Caps**: For larger stones or beads, use bead caps or additional wire wraps to secure them and help with alignment.

10. **Project Doesn't Look as Expected**

Problem: Sometimes, after all the hard work, the piece may not look as polished or visually appealing as you envisioned.

Solutions:

- **Review Your Plan**: Take a step back and review the design. Maybe you need to simplify the pattern or add an embellishment. Don't be afraid to make changes, even midway through the project.

- **Practice and Patience**: Wire weaving is a skill that improves over time. If the design doesn't look right, try again and apply the lessons you've learned.

Wire weaving can be challenging, but with patience and practice, you will overcome most problems that arise. Remember that each piece is an opportunity to learn, and don't be discouraged by mistakes—they're a natural part of the creative process. With these troubleshooting tips, you can address common problems and continue creating beautiful, intricate wire designs with confidence.

Conclusion

Wire weaving is a versatile and rewarding craft that combines creativity, patience, and technical skill to create intricate and beautiful jewelry pieces. From understanding the history and materials to mastering basic, intermediate, and advanced techniques, you now have the knowledge to embark on your wire weaving journey with confidence. By troubleshooting common issues and applying the tips for success, you can refine your craft and overcome challenges along the way.

As you continue to practice and experiment with different designs and materials, your skills will grow, allowing you to create unique and complex pieces that reflect your personal style. Whether you're a beginner or an experienced artisan, wire weaving offers endless opportunities for artistic expression and innovation. Embrace the learning process, enjoy the creativity, and let your imagination guide you in creating stunning wire-woven masterpieces. Happy weaving!

Made in the USA
Columbia, SC
31 May 2025

58737093R00054